CENGAGE Learning

# Drama for Students, Volume 2

*Staff*

David Galens and Lynn M. Spampinato, *Editors*

Thomas Allbaugh, Craig Bentley, Terry Browne, Christopher Busiel, Stephen Coy, L. M. Domina, John Fiero, Carol L. Hamilton, Erika Kreger, Jennifer Lewin, Sheri Metzger, Daniel Moran, Terry Nienhuis, Bonnie Russell, Arnold Schmidt, William Wiles, Joanne Woolway, *Contributing Writers*

Elizabeth Cranston, Kathleen J. Edgar, Joshua Kondek, Marie Lazzari, Tom Ligotti, Marie Napierkowski, Scot Peacock, Mary Ruby, Diane Telgen, Patti Tippett, Kathleen Wilson, Pam Zuber, *Contributing Editors*

Pamela Wilwerth Aue, *Managing Editor*

Jeffery Chapman, *Programmer/Analyst*

Victoria B. Cariappa, *Research Team Manager*
Michele P. LaMeau, Andy Guy Malonis, Barb

McNeil, Gary Oudersluys, Maureen Richards, *Research Specialists*
Julia C. Daniel, Tamara C. Nott, Tracie A. Richardson, Cheryl L. Warnock, *Research Associates*

Susan M. Trosky, *Permissions Manager*
Kimberly F. Smilay, *Permissions Specialist*
Sarah Chesney, *Permissions Associate*
Steve Cusack, Kelly A. Quin, *Permissions Assistants*

Mary Beth Trimper, *Production Director*
Evi Seoud, *Assistant Production Manager*
Shanna Heilveil, *Production Assistant*

Randy Bassett, *Image Database Supervisor*
Mikal Ansari, Robert Duncan, *Imaging Specialists*
Pamela A. Reed, *Photography Coordinator*

Cynthia Baldwin, *Product Design Manager*
Cover design: Michelle DiMercurio, *Art Director*
Page design: Pamela A. E. Galbreath, *Senior Art Director*

This book is printed on acid-free paper that meets the minimum requirements of American National Standard for Information Sciences—Permanence Paper for Printed Library Materials, ANSI Z39.48-1984.

ISBN 0-7876-1684-2

ISSN applied for and pending

Printed in the United States of America
10 9 8 7 6 5 4 3

# Long Day's Journey into Night

**Eugene O'Neill**

**1956**

## Introduction

Although Eugene O'Neill had completed *Long Day's Journey into Night* by 1941, it was not produced until 1956, three years after his death. He had originally stipulated that it was not to be produced or published until twenty-five years after he died. However, before his death he gave verbal permission to the Royal Dramatic Theatre to stage it in Stockholm, Sweden, a country that had accorded him a special loyalty throughout his career.

The Stockholm production, which opened on February 10, 1956, was very successful and prompted wide interest in the play. Nine months later, on November 7, the play opened to mixed but mostly favorable reviews at the Helen Hayes Theatre in New York. Featured in the cast were Frederic March as James Tyrone, Florence Eldridge as Mary, Jason Robards, Jr. as Jamie, Bradford Dilman as Edmund, and Katherine Ross as Cathleen. Jose Quintero both produced and directed the play.

Carlotta O'Neill, the playwright's widow, saw to the play's publication in the same year. In 1955 she had copyrighted the work as an unpublished play, and in the following year she asked Random House publish it. The editors declined, even though they held a sealed copy of the script that O'Neill had originally deposited with them. Mrs. O'Neill then offered the publication rights to the Yale Library, which arranged its release through the Yale University Press with the provision that the play royalties would be used to endow the Eugene O'Neill Memorial Fund at the Yale School of Drama. The published work met with great critical acclaim and won for O'Neill a fourth Pulitzer Prize.

# Author Biography

It was because *Long Day's Journey into Night* was so transparently autobiographical that Eugene O'Neill forbade the play's production and publication during his lifetime. The main characters are thinly veiled portraits of his father, James, his mother, Ella, his brother, Jamie, and himself.

James Gladstone O'Neill was born on October 6, 1888, in a Broadway hotel, son to the popular actor, James O'Neill, and Ella Quinlan. He was raised in the world of theater, and, as a result, in his boyhood and teen years he traveled all over America.

At eighteen, O'Neill entered Princeton but was expelled for a drunken prank and "general hell-raising." Thereafter he drifted. He served briefly as a business firm clerk, tried his hand at gold prospecting in Central America, and finally signed on a ship as an ordinary seaman in the Atlantic trade routes. After three years of wandering, he returned to New York, supporting himself with odd jobs and living on that city's squalid waterfront. In 1912, the year in which *Long Day's Journey into Night* is set, O'Neill broke off his three-year marriage to Kathleen Jenkins. In that same year, ill with tuberculosis and haunted by his "rebellious dissipations," he reached a personal low point and even attempted suicide.

While in a sanatorium recovering from

tuberculosis, O'Neill studied the master dramatists of the world and set out to become a playwright. Dissatisfied with his early efforts in the form, he enrolled at Harvard to study the craft, becoming the most celebrated member of George Pierce Baker's famous "47 Workshop." His first plays were published in 1914, and his first staged play, *Bound East for Cardiff,* was produced in 1916. It was followed by *Thirst,* produced by the Provincetown Players in the summer of 1917. It was that group that gave O'Neill his artistic arena and, with its move to New York, quickly established his reputation as the chief innovator in theater.

O'Neill then began a very prolific stretch of writing that lasted over a dozen years and vaulted him into the front rank of American playwrights. Through the 1920s, he penned a group of major plays, including *Beyond the Horizon* (1920), *The Emperor Jones* (1920), *Anna Christie* (1921), *The Hairy Ape* (1922), *All God's Chiliun Got Wings* (1924), *Desire Under the Elms* (1924), *The Great God Brown* (1926), *Strange Interlude* (1926), *Lazarus Laughed* (1928), *Dynamo* (1929), and *Mourning Becomes Electra* (1931).

O'Neill's personal grief helped shape his dramatic vision. Between 1920 and 1923, O'Neill's father, mother, and brother all died, leaving him deeply troubled. He attempted only one comedy, *Ah, Wilderness* (1933), concentrating instead on the grimmer side of life and relying heavily on the probing psychoanalytical theories of Sigmund Freud. He also mined his own life for his themes and characters, most obviously in his later plays, in which he clearly attempted to exorcise his subconscious familial guilt and sorrow.

O'Neill's reputation in the United States went into something of a decline after 1930, perhaps because his vigorous innovation and experimentation gave way to more morose autobiographical studies, some of which were not staged at the time. His international reputation remained high, however, and in 1936 he won the Nobel Prize in literature, only the second American at the time to have been so honored.

O'Neill and his third wife, Carlotta, went into relative seclusion in the late 1930s. Thereafter, in the 1940s, he was stricken with a degenerative neurological tremor which impaired his faculties and prevented him from undertaking new projects or completing work on his ambitious cycle of plays tentatively entitled "A Tale of Possessor Self-Dispossessed." However, he finished *Long Day's Journey into Night*, which many critics deem his crowning achievement. In the work's dedication to Carlotta, O'Neill indicated that he was finally able to pay homage to his family, the "four haunted Tyrones," and to write about his past "with deep pity and understanding and forgiveness."

In his last active years, O'Neill finished plays that now rank among his very best, including *The Iceman Cometh* (1946) and *A Moon for the Misbegotten* (1947). Other later plays include *A Touch of the Poet* (1957) and *Hughie* (1959), which, like *Long Day's Journey into Night*, were first produced posthumously. By the time he died in 1953, O'Neill had written over thirty significant dramatic works and solidified his reputation as America's premier dramatist.

# Plot Summary

*Long Day's Journey into Night* is set in the living room of the Tyrones' shoreline summer home in New London, Connecticut, in August of 1912. The play begins in the morning and ends late at night on the same day.

The work is divided into four acts. It largely consists of painful disclosures and acrimonious exchanges among the four family members, as major crises mount and finally engulf the family in despair. Of central concern are Mary's relapse into morphine addiction, Jamie's continued descent into irreversible dissipation, and Edmund's grim discovery that he has tuberculosis and must enter a sanatorium.

## *Act One*

The play, which opens just after breakfast, begins on a hopeful note, evident in the affectionate exchange between James and Mary Tyrone, but it is clear that Mary is being carefully watched by her family. Neither her morphine addiction nor Edmund's obvious ill health are honestly discussed. Instead, the characters fence around the truth with evasive banter, though, at times, resentment and disappointment surface. Tyrone upbraids Jamie, his eldest son, for encouraging Edmund, the younger son, to follow in Jamie's dissolute footsteps. Jamie, ever critical of "the Old Man," in turn derides

Tyrone as a miser, ultimately to blame for Mary's addiction and Edmund's ill health because of his penny-pinching reluctance to pay for competent doctors. To die father and sons, it becomes obvious that Mary is growing unstable, but she blames her edginess on a lack of sleep caused by Tyrone's snoring and the foghorn that sounded throughout the previous night. After the men leave to take up outside chores, Mary sinks into an armchair, clearly in a state of nervous agitation that threatens the last vestiges of her self-control.

## Act Two, Scene One

The scene opens just before lunch. Edmund and Jamie sneak some of their father's whiskey and men resort to Jamie's usual trick of watering the remaining whiskey to disguise their actions. Their discussion shifts from Edmund's health to their fears about their mother, and Jamie grows distraught because Edmund has let Mary stay upstairs by herself. When she enters, it is evident to both of mem that she has succumbed to the drug, smashing their hopes that she had finally shaken herself free of it. Jamie's sneering remarks about his father anger Mary, who excuses her husband's stinginess as the result of his hard life. She also fends off Jamie's insinuation that she has lapsed into her addiction again. Tyrone enters, and he soon realizes what has happened. After his sons exit for lunch, he remains behind with Mary, angry and defeated by her condition.

## Act Two, Scene Two

The family returns to the living room after lunch. A telephone call from Dr. Hardy confirms the diagnosis of Edmund's sickness as tuberculosis. Edmund must keep an afternoon appointment with Hardy. Although the full truth remains hidden from Mary, her verbal attack on Hardy indicates that she knows that Edmund suffers from more than "a summer cold." She leaves to go upstairs, and it is clear to the rest that she is going to use more morphine. The father-son recriminations begin again, with Tyrone accusing both Jamie and Edmund of abandoning their Catholic faith to embrace damning alternatives: in Jamie's case, degeneracy, and in Edmund's, a gloomy and self-destructive philosophy. Edmund leaves and Jamie warns his father not to put Edmund in a second-rate sanatorium, prone as he is to look for the cheapest way out. Mary returns and, left alone with Tyrone, complains about her loneliness and Tyrone's tightfisted failure to provide a real home. She bitterly blames Tyrone's lifestyle for past disasters, including her difficult birthing of Edmund and postpartum pain, then begins to drift into the solace of her romanticized past, when she was in a convent school planning to become a nun or a concert pianist. Edmund returns and pleads with her to stop taking the morphine, but it is clearly to no avail. She can only try to make him stop blaming himself for her renewed addiction.

## Act Three

It is early evening, and Mary has sunk further into her drug-induced detachment from reality, which, like the gathering fog outside, "hides you from the world." She is alone with Cathleen, the servant who had accompanied her on her automobile ride into town to obtain more morphine. She confides in the girl, treating her like a childhood friend while plying her with Tyrone's whiskey. She tells the servant about her early hopes and her romanticized first impressions of Tyrone. After Cathleen leaves to resume her duties, Tyrone and Edmund enter. Both have been drinking and continue to imbibe while Mary drifts through a reverie on Jamie's alcoholism, her early married life on the itinerant hotel-hopping theater circuit, and her expensive satin wedding gown. When Tyrone leaves to fetch another bottle of whiskey, Edmund tries to tell his mother that he must enter a sanatorium, but she refuses to accept the truth, which, because her own father had died of consumption, she fears is a virtual death sentence. He voices wounding regret that he has "a dope fiend for a mother," but is immediately contrite and hurries away. The act ends in a confrontation between Mary and Tyrone over Edmund's condition. Mary refuses to eat dinner, claiming she is tired, and Tyrone then accuses her of slipping off to "take more of that God-damned poison."

## Act Four

It is around midnight. Tyrone, morose and almost lost in an alcoholic stupor, awkwardly attempts to play solitaire. Edmund enters, also drunk, and is immediately accused of "burning up money" by leaving the lights on behind him. Edmund attempts to defy his father, and is quick to defend his brother against his father's ritual complaints about Jamie's debauchery. Edmund then launches into a self-pitying conceit about being "a ghost within a ghost," a soul lost in the comfort of the fog. His father only finds him morbid. Edmund continues, reciting depressing poetry and fueling his father's anger. They begin to play Casino, but they are constantly distracted from the cards by their concern for Jamie and their fear that Mary will get up and come downstairs. They also continue to drink, reflect on their lives, and trade a mixture of recriminations and affectionate concerns for each other. They discuss Mary and her romantic distortions of the truth about her earlier life in the convent and her father's wealth. Edmund then takes up Jamie's theme of Tyrone's stinginess, evident in Tyrone's effort to find an inexpensive sanatorium for Edmund. Tyrone offers his familiar excuse, arguing that his family poverty and experience as a child laborer instilled in him a desperate fear of the poor house, turning him into "a stinking old miser." He reveals his own deep regret that his fears led him to sacrifice his acting talent for a fixed but secure and very lucrative role in a popular melodrama. Edmund, in his turn, laments the loss of hope found in rare moments at sea, where life, however briefly, seemed to hold some meaning.

Jamie, drunk, lurches through the house and into the room as Tyrone, to avoid a confrontation, retires to the side porch. After recounting his adventure with Fat Violet in a local brothel, Jamie begins a painful confession in which he claims that his bitter resentment towards Edmund has caused him to try to drag Edmund into his own moral quicksand and turn him into a bum. He admits to having been jealous of Edmund and holding him responsible for Mary's addiction. His love for his kid brother, though stronger than the hate, will not stop him from wanting to see Edmund fail.

When Jamie seems to fall asleep, Tyrone returns and begins his litany of complaints about his oldest son, but he is interrupted when Jamie starts up and begins returning fire with caustic, sneering innuendos.

The men, worn down by drink and a lack of sleep, soon begin to doze, but they quickly grow alert when they hear the piano begin a badly rendered Chopin waltz in a nearby room. Mary, carrying her wedding gown on her arm, then makes the entrance the men have dreaded. She is obviously in a narcotic-induced trance, barely aware of her surroundings. She begins a detached and vacant reverie on her childhood dreams and hopes. The men remain immobilized, making only feeble attempts to break through to her, vainly reciting lines of verse that underscore the helplessness of their situation. Mary's reverie continues as the men sit quietly in their chairs and an indifferent curtain finally descends.

# Characters

## *Cathleen*

The "second girl," Cathleen is the Tyrone household maid, "a buxom Irish peasant" of about Edmund's age. She is dull, awkward, and slow but very amiable and totally unaffected. She shows no awareness that her familiarity is inappropriate for a servant, and her ingenuousness encourages Mary to treat her almost like an old school chum and confidant.

## *Gaspard*

*See* James Tyrone

## *Jamie*

*See* James Tyrone, Jr.

## *The Kid*

*See* Edmund Tyrone

## *The Old Man*

*See* James Tyrone

## *Edmund Tyrone*

Edmund, the youngest son of James and Mary Tyrone, is twenty-three, ten years younger than his brother, Jamie. Thinner, and a bit taller than Jamie, Edmund more closely resembles his mother than his father. He also shares some of his mother's nervousness, evident in his hands. A fledgling journalist, he is also a poet. He is more of an intellectual than his brother and quickly becoming better read, but he has also seen something of the world, working on merchant ships as a common seaman and drifting through waterfront bars and flophouses. He has a deep and abiding love of the sea, but he also has a morbid view of life that his father finds deeply distressing. He has a special bond with Jamie, for whom he has a great affection. He is ill with tuberculosis, and the consumptive disease is evident in his gaunt frame, wracking cough, and sallow complexion.

## James Tyrone

The sixty-five year old family patriarch, James Tyrone is a financially successful and handsome actor whose robust looks and bearing and make him appear more youthful. His popular success has not spoiled him, partly because he is a self-made man from a poor immigrant Irish family deserted by his father. His resulting fear of poverty has turned him into a man obsessed with money and owning property, always looking for bargains, even at the expense of his family's health. From that same heritage comes a lack of snobbery and pretension. He wears clothes to "the limit of usefulness," and thus appears somewhat shabby and careless in his dress. However, he does reveal the "studied technique" of an experienced actor and takes some pride in his powerful, resonant voice and his command of language. His wife's morphine addiction and his sons' profligate lives have made him both resentful and angry. Whiskey offers him some solace, but he is never able to escape the recrimination of his sons, who hold him partly responsible for their mother's drug addiction.

# Media Adaptations

- *Long Day's Journey into Night* was first adapted to film by Sidney Lumet, and starred Katharine Hepburn, Sir Ralph Richardson, Jason Robards, Jr., and Dean Stockwell. A black and white film, Embassy, 1962; available from Republic Pictures Home Video.

- *Long Day's Journey into Night* was produced again as a made for television film by Jonathan Miller, using Sinclair Lewis's adaptation of the play, and starring Peter Gallagher, Jack Lemmon, Bethel Leslie, and Kevin Spacey, in 1988; available from Lorimar Home Video/Vestron.

- A third version of the play, filmed at the Tom Patterson Theatre in Stratford, Ontario, Canada, was directed by David Wellington, and starred Peter Donaldson, Martha Henry, William Hutt, and Tom McCamus, Stratford Festival, 1996; not currently available.

---

## James Tyrone, Jr.

The oldest son of James and Mary Tyrone, Jamie, at thirty-three, shows the physical signs of his dissipation. He favors his father in appearance, but lacks the Old Man's robust vitality and graceful presence. He is an unabashed and unapologetic drunk, with a history of failing at most everything he has tried. He is also a womanizer, spending much of his time haunting saloons and brothels. Afflicted with a caustic cynicism and sneering manner, he mocks his father at every turn, blaming Tyrone's miserly ways for most of the family problems.

Though protective towards Edmund, he admits to a desire to corrupt him, to shape his brother in his own image, and he knows why. His beloved mother's use of morphine had begun after bearing Edmund, and a part of Jamie hates his brother as the source of her pain. For Tyrone, Jamie is nothing but a free-loading, ungrateful bum, quickly slipping beyond redemption. Jamie is at least honest enough to agree with that assessment of his character.

## *Mary Tyrone*

Mary, wife to James Tyrone, at fifty-four, is several years younger than her husband. She is described as having a "graceful figure" with a distinctly Irish face, once pretty and "still striking." From the outset, it is clear that she is on edge, nervously fluttering her fingers, once beautiful but now gnarled by rheumatism. She has been addicted to morphine for several years, and has been in out of sanitariums, desperately trying to get free of her dependency. Under the influence of the drug, she escapes into an idealized version of her girlhood at a convent school, with dreams of becoming a nun or a concert pianist. She finds the real world lonely and depressing, offering little hope or joy. She cannot deal with unpleasant truths; for example, that her son Edmund might be suffering from something more serious than a cold. Still, she retains the "unaffected charm" and "innate unworldly innocence" of her youth, explaining her family's protective loyalty and love and crushing disappointment when she once more falls victim to her addiction.

# Themes

The plot of *Long Day's Journey into Night* focuses on a dysfunctional family trying to come to grips with its ambivalent emotions in the face of serious familial problems, including drug addiction, moral degradation, deep-rooted fear and guilt, and life-threatening illness.

## *Alienation and Loneliness*

The Tyrone family is fragmented, and each of its members to some degree is alienated from the rest. The most obvious estrangement exists between Tyrone and Jamie, both of whom allow their bitterness to overwhelm whatever residual love and respect they have for each other. Jamie holds his father's tightfistedness to blame for Mary's addiction to morphine, while Tyrone cannot forgive what he sees as his son's gutter-bound dissolution. The two are barely civil to each other, and knowing the recriminations their encounters habitually bring, they simply try to avoid each other, especially when drink has dissolved their masks of civility.

More subtle is the ambivalent alienation that Jamie feels towards Edmund. He confesses that a part of him hates Edmund, from jealousy and an irrational association of Edmund's survival with their mother's desperate plight.

Most estranged and alienated of all is Mary.

Her struggle with her addiction is desperately lonely, most of the time beyond the others' understanding or sympathy. She talks at length of her isolation, placing much blame on Tyrone for the itinerant life his acting career imposed on them. Under the influence of morphine, Mary drifts into her idealized past, cut off from the pain of her current life.

## Deception

Deceptive masks are worn early in the play in an effort to evade unpleasant truths. The other members of the family try to keep Mary from knowing that Edmund is seriously ill, and Mary obviously attempts to deceive herself with the comforting belief that Edmund is only suffering from "a summer cold." Mary also attempts to hide her relapse into drug use with pathetic excuses that simply deepen the family's disappointment. The deceptions even become trivial, in Jamie's efforts to deceive his father by watering down the whiskey, for example, or in Tyrone's efforts to hide his whiskey-fetching forays from the help.

More poignant are the self-deceptions, in which characters mask the truth from themselves. Clearly, the past into which Mary escapes is illusory, a romanticized but comforting distortion of truth. Even Jamie, cynical but honest, deludes himself in his search for personal redemption through alcoholism and whoring.

# God and Religion

For Tyrone, a troubling problem is his sons' rejection of their Catholic faith, a foundation stone in their "shanty Irish" heritage. His complaints about their rejection of religion occasions Jamie's scoffing observation that Tyrone himself is a truant Catholic, which Tyrone must admit. He insists, though, that he still believes in God, which his sons do not. He is particularly upset with Edmund's godless and pessimistic view of life, claiming that it has been learned from reading depressing, atheistic poetry and philosophy.

# Guilt and Innocence

Mary's illusory, drug-induced escape into her youth is partly a flight from guilt into a restored innocence and rediscovered faith. In their own ways, the other Tyrones try to unburden themselves of guilt and shame, either through expiation, as seen in Jamie's admission of his jealousy of Edmund, or in pleas for understanding, as seen in Tyrone's attempts to blame his selfish penny pinching on his early poverty. The play's tragic theme is that innocence can not be restored; each character must bear some guilt and pain, even to the grave's edge.

# Loyalty

The loyalty of the three Tyrone men towards Mary has eroded because she has repeatedly dashed their hopes for her recovery, but their anger, hurt, and disappointment are an emotional index of their love for her. It is the common loyalty towards her that keeps the family together and explains why, for example, Jamie and Tyrone even tolerate each other.

## Memory and Reminiscence

Mary is not the only one with regrets about the past. Tyrone is haunted by his impoverished childhood and his father's abandonment and eventual suicide. In one self-pitying confession, he expresses regrets for having given up the chance of becoming a great Shakespearean actor in order to take a lucrative but artistically unrewarding part in a popular melodrama.

## Moral Corruption

Implicit in the responses to Mary's drug addiction is the belief that addiction was an indication of a weak moral will. Public disclosure of her behavior seems to be more threatening to the family than Jamie's disgraceful drinking, gambling, and whoring. In honest moments, Tyrone recognizes that the morphine is a poison and that Mary cannot control her need, but the moral stigma remains. Jamie's moral descent, buffered by his affection for his brother and mother, is treated as less of a social embarrassment, even by Tyrone.

## Search for Self

The principal searcher in *Long Day's Journey into Night* is Edmund, O'Neill's alter ego. Both Mary and Tyrone escape to their pasts, Mary to her convent days and Tyrone to a time in his career when he might have resisted trading his talent for wealth. Edmund, having just begun a writing career as a poet and journalist, looks to a future when his drifting ends and he finds an elusive inner peace that he has glimpsed in rare moments at sea. The alternative is to follow Jamie, his dissolute doppelganger, down a self-destructive, unhappy path to a spiritual dead end.

## *Wealth and Poverty*

Throughout *Long Day's Journey into Night,* Tyrone confirms the justice of Jamie's sneering attacks on him as a miser. Old Gaspard, as Jamie calls him, is obsessed with the cost of things, and is always looking for the cheapest alternative. He invariably equates the best with a bargain price, whether he is buying land, cigars, or automobiles, employing servants, or engaging the services of a physician.

On occasion, Tyrone's penny-pinching habits border on the comic. He cannot resist remarking on the most trivial of his marketplace triumphs, and he launches into diatribes about making the electric company rich while he wanders through the house turning off lights in rooms that others have abandoned. But there is real pathos, too, for some of the family problems have their origin in Tyrone's misplaced values, which, in an honest moment, even he admits. Jamie never lets him forget that it was his reluctance to seek out a competent physician that led to Mary's addiction. Jamie fears, too, that Tyrone will attempt to find a bargain sanatorium for Edmund, and repeatedly warns his father against doing so.

# Topics for Further Study

- Investigate the history of the use of morphine and the problems of morphine addiction from the time of its chemical isolation from opium in 1806 to the present day.

- Research the development of sanatoria or hospitals devoted to consumptive diseases and their methods of treating tuberculosis prior to the development of modern vaccines and chemotherapy.

- Investigate the plight of Irish Catholic immigrants to America at the time of the potato blight famine that struck Europe in 1845.

- Select one or more of the poets, novelists, or playwrights mentioned or quoted in the play and investigate their literary legacy and influence on O'Neill.

- Research the state of the American theater at the end of the nineteenth century, particularly the negative effect that the profit motives of commercial theaters had on the quality of their productions.

---

Indirectly, Tyrone begs for understanding, even forgiveness, by recounting his hard beginnings in an Irish immigrant family, deserted by his father. His fears of landing in the poorhouse are honest enough, for they relate to that dreadful time, when he had to work twelve hours a day in a machine shop to help his family survive. Tyrone has little success in engaging his sons' sympathies, however. Although Edmund claims to understand his father better, both sons are weary of his stories and are largely indifferent to his past; their concern is with the end result of Tyrone's stinginess, not its cause.

*Long Day's Journey into Night* is Eugene O'Neill's thinly veiled autobiographical study of a dysfunctional family disintegrating because of its inability to cope with drug addiction, life-threatening illness, shame, and guilt.

## Dramatic Unities

Throughout the four acts of *Long Day's Journey into Night,* O'Neill preserves the unities of time and place. The setting remains the living room of the Tyrone's summer home in New London, Connecticut, and, in emulation of the classical practice, the action unfolds within a single day in August of 1912, starting in the early morning and ending around midnight. Each scene and act is a segment of that single day, and within each the progress of time is scrupulously faithful to the passage of real world time, relentless and impersonal.

## Symbolism

O'Neill, within the realistic limits of his drama, uses symbolism very effectively. Of fundamental significance is the fog. It serves first as a mood enhancing but wholly natural phenomenon. At the beginning of the play, the fog of the night before has lifted, and the optimism of the Tyrone family is reflected in the day's early brightness. But by dinner time in Act Three, the fog has again rolled in, its presence announced by a foghorn "moaning like a mournful whale in labor." Its return suits the encroaching sense of futility and isolation of each of the main characters, particularly Mary. It is she who asks why the "fog makes everything sound so sad and lost."

At a more complex symbolic level, the fog has further significance. It is evoked as a metaphor in the rhapsodic self-scrutiny of Edmund, for example. Confiding in his father, Edmund claims that he desires to melt into the fog, to "be alone with myself in another world where truth is untrue and life can hide from itself," to become "a ghost belonging to the fog."

The fog is also a place of forgetfulness, a place where reality is dimmed, and the world is oddly distorted. It thus serves as a symbol of Mary's drug-induced stupor and her escape into an idealized past that offers her a brief respite from pain.

## *Autobiographical Elements*

The "haunted Tyrones" are dramatic portraits of O'Neill's real family, and the events of the play reflect a critical time in his life when he was about to enter a sanatorium with a mild case of tuberculosis. Like James Tyrone, O'Neill's father, James O'Neill, had been a highly successful actor, famous in the role of Edmund Dantes in a stage adaptation of Alexandre Dumas's *Count of Monte*

*Cristo*. Like Mary, O'Neill's mother, Ella Quinlan, became addicted to morphine under circumstances that may have been like those described in the play. And, like Jamie, O'Neill's older brother was an alcoholic and struggling actor who literally drank himself to death after Ella O'Neill died of cancer. Many of the play's details are also rooted in fact, including the New London setting and the Tyrone family history.

## *Allusions*

Although the drama is not rich in allusions to public events of the time, it does use references to several writers and often includes parts of poems and character references and lines from dramatic works woven into the dialogue. While the furniture in the living room is both sparse and shabby, its two bookcases are filled with volumes of writers past and present, carefully named by O'Neill in his stage directions and mentioned in the dialogue. Tyrone's preference is for Shakespeare, who is often quoted, while Edmund's is for more modern writers and philosophers, like Nietzsche, Dowson, Marx, Baudelaire, and Swinburne, writers that his father finds gloomy, morally repugnant, or anarchistic. Jamie, too, has read his share of literature. In the final act, it is he who quotes several lines from Swinburne's "A Leave Taking" in choric counterpoint to Mary's painful monologue.

Allusion is also made to the famous American actor, Edwin Booth. It is a point of great pride for

Tyrone that he had once acted on stage with Booth, who thought highly of Tyrone's skill. But the memory is painful, for Tyrone is plagued by the belief that he traded his talent short for easy money.

## *Foreshadowing*

*Long Day's Journey into Night* begins cheerfully enough. The day is bright, and the initial exchanges between Tyrone and Mary are affectionate and playful, but foreboding clues to the play's tragic turn are quickly introduced. Mary's behavior hints at her return to morphine use. We learn that she had spent a sleepless night and that her appetite is poor. She is obviously restless. She also seems slightly disoriented, even mildly hysterical. Her fluttering hands and obsessive concern with her hair, her inability to find her glasses—all these foreshadow her mounting loss of self-control.

## *Monologue*

Lengthy monologues are used in *Long Day's Journey into Night* in at least two important ways: as reveries and confessions. Central are the reveries of Mary. As she plunges deeper into her drug-induced daze, she rambles on about the past into which she desperately wants to escape. At times she seems incoherent; she even babbles. In her final appearance, she begins a long, inchoate monologue, almost totally oblivious to the efforts of other characters to break through to her. Edmund's long poetic discourse on fog is both a sort of confession and a reverie, as is Tyrone's monologue on his earlier life in theater. Almost pure confession is Jamie's meandering fourth act monologue in which he starts explaining why he stayed with Fat Violet and ends with his admission that he has tried to corrupt Edmund.

## Naturalism

Naturalism, which espouses a clinical approach in literature, is noted for its "slice of life" action lines. Such fiction often lacks closure, remaining open-plotted and inconclusive. Problems, like those in *Long Day's Journey into Night,* are left unresolved, hanging on and dragging the characters into an implied future beyond the scope of the work. Naturalistic works also tend to be grim. They strip away a character's sense of dignity to expose unpleasant truths that lie at uncomfortable depths, even below the character's conscious being. It is invariably a painful process, and it is one that is central to O'Neill's play.

## Oedipus Complex

Often noted is the Freudian influence on O'Neill, particularly his espousal of the Oedipal attachment of sons to their mothers and sexual jealousy and enmity towards their fathers. Although a possible inner source of guilt in Edmund, the character whose behavior most clearly evidences a latent Oedipal guilt is Jamie. He seeks a surrogate mother among matronly prostitutes and reveals a bitter jealousy towards Edmund, his chief rival for Mary's affections in the Oedipal model outlined by Freud.

# Historical Context

There are two historical periods relevant to *Long Day's Journey into Night*. The play was written between 1939 and 1941, but it is set in 1912, at a critical period in the author's own life, paralleling that of his fictional persona, Edmund Tyrone.

## *Public Events*

Events of moment from the outside world do not intrude on the Tyrone family dialogue. For example, there is no mention of the April, 1912, sinking of the *Titanic,* which took over fifteen hundred passengers to their watery death, and was the greatest maritime disaster of the age. Nor is mention made of Captain Robert Scott's ill-fated expedition to the South Pole, which ended in March, 1912, when Scott and the last survivors died in a heroic attempt to reach awaiting shelter and provisions.

O'Neill's focus, relentlessly on the Tyrone family problems, simply made unnecessary the need for allusions to such important topical events. They are conspicuous only by their absence, a fact that contributes to the play's claustrophobic impact. An awareness of the outside world is reflected not in events but in the social consciousness of the Tyrones. They have a sense of living on the margins of respectability, not fully accepted by the "Yanks" because of Tyrone's impoverished, shanty-Irish,

Roman Catholic heritage.

For the audience there is a foreshadowing of the impending American love affair with the automobile, which Henry Ford made possible when he introduced the Model T in 1908. By 1913, his company was able to sell the model for $500, putting it within the financial reach of most middle-class families. Tyrone, bound by his past, dislikes the second-hand auto he has bought for Mary, and he expresses his preference for the trolley and walking. Only Mary uses the car, and she must be driven by a paid chauffeur, to Tyrone's tight-fisted consternation. Clearly, the world is passing Tyrone by, as in real life it seemed to be passing O'Neill's father by.

## *A Battle of the Books*

Two bookcases occupy the Tyrone living room. The first, small and plain, contains works by modern writers, many of them favorites of Edmund and Jamie: novels by Balzac, Zola, and Stendhal; plays by Ibsen, Shaw, and Strindberg; poetry by Rossetti, Wilde, Dowson, and Kipling; and philosophical works by Nietzsche, Marx, Engels, and Schopenhauer. The second, larger, glass-fronted bookcase contains older works, including three sets of Shakespeare, sets of die romantic fiction of Dumas and Victor Hugo, fifty imposing volumes of the world's greatest literature, several major works of history and miscellaneous old plays, poetry collections, and Irish histories. This second, more venerable appearing bookcase contains the preferred readings of James Tyrone, Sr. There is but one common link: Shakespeare's picture adorns the wall above the plainer bookcase, implying that he holds a place of honor even in the hearts of the sons.

# Compare & Contrast

- **1910s:** World War I begins in the summer of 1914, with the United States joining the allies against Germany in 1917.

  **1940s and 50s:** O'Neill finishes *Long Day's Journey into Night* prior to America's entry into World War II on December 7, 1941. The Cold War with the Soviet bloc flares into open combat in Korea, a "police action" ending with an armistice agreement signed on July 27, 1953, four months before O'Neill dies. In 1956 the Soviet Union cracks down on dissidents in Poland and Hungary; that same year *Long Day's Journey into Night* wins O'Neill, posthumously, his final Pulitzer Prize.

  **Today:** The 1990s bring an end to the Cold War and to fears of a nuclear holocaust.

- **1910s:** The airplane, automobile,

and motion pictures, all in their infancy, begin a radical transformation of daily American life.

**1940s and 50s:** Films, with sound since 1928, are the most popular entertainment medium; commercial airlines continue to replace trains in distance passenger travel; and American houses start sporting double garages. By the 1950s, television becomes both popular and increasingly affordable; jet engines become common on commercial planes; and large finned automobiles with powerful engines streak through America on a growing network of parkways and highways.

**Today:** Houses without at least two television sets grow rare; railroads continue a losing struggle to survive; and automobiles, while legally moving faster on interstate highways again, get smaller, more fuel-efficient, and ever more expensive.

- **1910s:** America begins reflecting an awareness of foreign movements in art and letters, of the French naturalists like Zola and Balzac, and the realistic drama of Ibsen, Strindberg, and Chekhov; O'Neill reveals that foreign influence in his very first plays.

**1940s and 50s:** American readers remain drawn to the fiction of William Faulkner, Ernest Hemingway, John Steinbeck, and F. Scott Fitzgerald; the plays of Clifford Odets, Maxwell Anderson, Lillian Hellman, and Robert Sherwood also have a dedicated following, but O'Neill's reputation remains stagnant. By the 1950s, a host of postwar novelists and poets make their mark, challenging Faulkner and Hemingway, Frost and Eliot, for book stall space; the realistic problem play reaches its maturity in the works of Arthur Miller, Tennessee Williams, William Inge, and O'Neill, while avant garde rumblings are heard in the Off-and Off-Off Broadway wings.

**Today:** Laurels in fiction are up for grabs; in theater, August Wilson, Sam Shepard, and David Mamet continue making an indelible mark.

- **1910s:** Through stricter federal laws governing drug use and the militant success of the Anti-Saloon League and the Women's Christian Temperance Union, America seeks to end drug addiction and alcohol abuse; achieves Prohibition with ratification of the Eighteenth Amendment in 1919.

**1940s and 50s:** With prohibition repealed in 1933, America returns to imbibing alcohol, creating a new, post-World War II problem: the drunk driver; morphine still widely used as a pain killer. The Beat Generation brings "mind expanding" drugs like marijuana closer to the mainstream; middle-class America turns to tranquilizers to cope with depression; hard drugs begin to plague the inner cities; synthetics like methadone replace morphine in some medical applications.

**Today:** Drug abuse remains a major problem, with crack cocaine and heroin an inner-city blight and marijuana use common everywhere in America, especially among the young; groups like Mothers Against Drunk Driving (MADD) help stiffen penalties for driving while under the influence, in some states upgrading repeat offenses to a felony.

---

The rift that separates Tyrone and his sons, though firmly based in familial guilt and shame, has been widened by their disparate tastes in literature and philosophy. Throughout the play, literary allusions and quotations provide a dominant recurring theme in the emotionally charged rounds of repeated accusation and counter accusation. Clearly, Edmund's taste is for die realists and naturalists in fiction and drama, materialists and nihilists in philosophy, and fatalists and adherents to the detached, art-for-art's-sake school in poetry.

Tyrone finds Edmund's tastes deplorable, writers full of nothing but gloom and despair. He dismisses the lot of them as decadent, depressing, and godless. For him, Shakespeare reigns supreme. He even has a theory that the real Shakespeare was not English but an Irish Catholic.

O'Neill's real father, like Tyrone, was one of the last of the matinee idols, working in a theater that admitted little that was new or unconventional. Typical fare was warmed-over Shakespeare and heroic melodrama, works that provided lucrative vehicles for popular actors like James O'Neill but insulated the theater from the real world. Eugene O'Neill would change all that; influenced by the writers whose works rest on Edmund's bookcase, by the 1920s he would revolutionize the American theater.

## Substance Abuse: Morphine and Alcohol

By 1912, responsible physicians had stopped the indiscriminate use of morphine as a pain killer and treatment for depression. New laws required pharmacists to dispense it only by authorized prescription, ending its unrestricted use. However, for many Americans like Mary Tyrone, the damage had already been done. Morphine and laudanum, another opium derivative, had left thousands addicted, and many faced the social stigma and disgrace that drug addiction finally involved.

The excessive use of alcohol was more widely tolerated, at least in men. The saloon was an established American institution by the end of the nineteenth century. It served as a working man's social club where males could imbibe, discuss the day's events, and wager on cards and billiards. Some of the saloons were also haunts for prostitutes, while others were outright bordellos; most, like their English pub counterparts, did not admit ladies.

Many saloon patrons, like Jamie Tyrone, were problem drinkers and gamblers, prone to violence, sexual promiscuity, or insolvency. Their excesses fueled the temperance reform movement, led and supported by a growing legion of women who wanted to protect families from "demon rum" and improve the nation's moral character and health. The movement would finally win a legal victory in 1919 with the passage and ratification of the Eighteenth Amendment. But the victory proved hollow. The ban on alcohol gave rise to illegal bootlegging, bathtub gin, and the infamous speakeasy, a Jazz Age substitute for the old saloon. Unlike the saloon, the speakeasies were patronized by men and the new generation of liberated "flappers," setting the model for the bars and nightclubs that went into legal operation when prohibition ended.

## Tuberculosis

Tuberculosis, called "consumption" by the Tyrones, was a dread disease in 1912, claiming close to 100,000 American lives annually. Treatment, provided in special hospitals called sanatoria, was largely in an experimental stage of development. Although physicians knew that a germ caused the disease, they had no miracle cure. A few used x-ray treatments, but most tried to counter the disease's symptoms with prolonged rest, special diets, and an abundance of fresh air. Edmund, who discovers that he has consumption, faces a period of recovery in a sanatorium, just as O'Neill himself did in 1912.

## The Great Depression

Prohibition ended in 1933, a half dozen years before O'Neill started writing *Long Day's Journey into Night*. Throughout the 1930s, America suffered a deep economic depression from which it had not completely recovered by the time O'Neill began the play. Although O'Neill's political sympathies were with the working class, he wrote what has been termed "private tragedy," not social-conscience polemics like Clifford Odets's *Waiting for Lefty* (1935) and other works of the leftist Group Theatre. In the 1930s, O'Neill's reputation went into a decline, despite the fact that he won the Nobel Prize for literature in 1936.

## *World War II*

World War II commenced in 1939, when Nazi Germany invaded Poland. Two years later, on December 7, 1941, the United States entered the war when the Japanese bombed Pearl Harbor. Fortunately, by that time O'Neill had finished *Long Day's Journey into Night*. The War's impact and his declining health brought his writing to a near standstill. In 1943, in the middle of the war, O'Neill and Carlotta burned the fragmentary parts of his projected cycle of plays, which by then he knew he would never finish.

# Critical Overview

In 1956, the production of *Long Day's Journey into Night* by the Royal Dramatic Theatre in Sweden won much praise for O'Neill. Potential producers soon pressured Carlotta O'Neill to release the work for an American staging, and after several months she turned the play over to Jose Quintero and two associates. Quintero's earlier revival of *The Iceman Cometh,* which opened in May of 1956, had already prompted new enthusiasm for O'Neill. His New York production of *Long Day's Journey into Night,* coupled with the play's publication by the Yale University Press, fully elevated O'Neill's reputation and restored him to the front ranks of American dramatists.

Leading critics like Brooks Atkinson, Walter Kerr, Harold Clurman, and Joseph Wood Krutch proclaimed the play's power on stage. Kerr, for example, in his review in the *New York Herald Tribune,* called the play "a stunning theatrical experience," while *New York Times* critic Atkinson announced that with the production of *Long Day's Journey into Night* the American theater had reached "stature and size." But the critical vindication of O'Neill was not unanimous. Some reviewers subtly condemned the work with tepid praise. Others pondered the play's stage power in the face of what Stephen Whicher, reviewing the Stockholm production for *Commonweal,* claimed were "several massive faults which should have destroyed it." Yet others paraded out old complaints about the playwright's heavy handed, awkward technique, tortured dialogue, painful self-flagellation, oppressive length, and morbid pessimism. One reviewer, Gilbert Seldes, commenting on the published play in *Saturday Review,* faulted the playwright's repetition, long speeches, "passion for reciting poetry," and his "desperate flatness of language." Another commentator, the *New Yorker's* Wolcott Gibbs, complained that the play "is often as barbarously written as it is possible for the work of a major writer to be," and doubted the work's status "as a major contribution to the drama of our time."

The unabashed autobiographical content of *Long Day's Journey into Night* also troubled many critics, some of whom argued that the play simply failed to evoke die emotions appropriate to tragedy because, as C. J. Rolo maintained in the *Atlantic Monthly*, the characters were "not only devoid of heroic attributes" but "even lacking in ordinary dignity and strength." For Rolo, the play failed to produce what O'Neill himself referred to as the "transfiguring nobility of tragedy."

Artistically, O'Neill, a tireless innovator, always had to swim against some pretty strong critical currents. Noting what seem like obvious flaws in his work, some important critics have only grudgingly agreed to O'Neill's status as the dean American theater. There is, for example, Eric Bentley's famous quip: "He is the leading American playwright; damn him, damn all; and damning all is a big responsibility." Bentley's frustration with O'Neill partly stems from what has always bedeviled O'Neill's critics—the fact that his texts never seem to suggest the grandeur that their dramatizations often achieve on stage. Away from the magic of theater, under a reader's naked light, his plays can sometimes seem pedestrian and awkward, almost embarrassingly so.

That fact has made some writers circumspect in approaching O'Neill's published plays. Harold Clurman, reviewing the Yale text of *Long Day's Journey into Night* in the *Nation,* remarked that "O'Neill's plays are nearly always more impressive on the stage than on the printed page." O'Neill was "a faulty craftsman," perhaps, but, as Clurman noted, the Swedish production had held its audience transfixed for four and one-half hours, a performance length that modern audiences would normally find unendurable, barely tolerable in a great classic like Shakespeare's *Hamlet*, which litters the stage with corpses, but not in a play in which there is very little overt action and nothing is really resolved.

The length and perplexing content of *Long Day's Journey into Night* hardly made it common fare in community, regional, or even academic theaters, thus its great power on stage was largely unknown in America's heartland until 1962, when Sidney Lumet's film version appeared. The movie, running under three hours, edited out some of the original play, but what remained was hailed as a remarkable cinematic triumph that remained essentially faithful to the Broadway production of the play. The film version must be credited with once again making O'Neill popular and with revealing to its wide audience the great force that lies, not just in, but around O'Neill's words.

As Travis Bogard observed in his book *Contour in Time: The Plays of Eugene O'Neill,* in *Long Day's Journey into Night* O'Neill managed "a return to four boards and a passion," placing great faith in his actors, the interpreters of his text. For Bogard and many other critics, O'Neill's last works are his greatest, "the highest achievement of the American realistic theatre," and of these *Long Day's Journey into Night* is indisputably regarded as the best.

# Sources

Atkinson, Brooks. Review of *Long Day's Journey into Night, New York Times,* Vol. 47, November 8, 1956, p. 2.

Bogard, Travis. *Contour in Time: The Plays of Eugene O'Neill,* revised edition, Oxford University Press, 1988.

Clurman, Harold. "The O'Neills," *Nation,* Vol. 182, March 3, 1956, pp. 182-83.

Falk, Doris V. *Eugene O'Neill and the Tragic Tension: An Interpretive Study of the Plays,* Rutgers University Press, 1958.

Gibbs, Wolcott. "Doom," *New Yorker,* Vol. 32, November 24, 1956, pp. 120-21.

Hewes, Henry. "O'Neill: 100 Proof—Not a Blend," *Saturday Review,* Vol. 39, November 2, 1961, pp. 30-1.

Hewes, Henry. "O'Neill and Faulkner via the Abroad Way," *Saturday Review,* Vol. 39, October 20, 1956, p. 58.

Kerr, Walter. Review of *Long Day's Journey into Night,* in *New York Herald-Tribune,* November 8, 1956.

Raleigh, John Henry. *The Plays of Eugene O'Neill,* Southern Illinois University Press, 1965.

Rolo, Charles J. "The Trouble of One House,"

*Atlantic Monthly,* Vol. 97, March, 1956, pp. 84-5.

Seldes, Gilbert. "Long day's Journey into Night," *Saturday Review,* Vol. 39, February 25, 1956, pp. 15-16.

Whicher, Stephen. "O'Neill's Long Journey," *Commonweal,* Vol. 63, March 16, 1956, pp. 614-15.

# Further Reading

Hayes, Richard. "A Requiem for Mortality," *Commonweal,* Vol. 64, February 1, 1957, pp. 467-68.

> A belated review of the Broadway production of *Long Day's Journey into Night* praising both the play and the cast for achieving "tragic nobility" within a realistic framework.

McDonnell, Thomas P. "O'Neill's Drama of the Psyche," *Catholic World,* Vol. 197, April, 1963, pp. 120-25.

> Argues that *Long Day's Journey into Night* is O'Neill's apotheosis in his quest for a tragedy of self, of his own tormented psyche.

Manheim, Michael. *Eugene O'Neill's New Language of Kinship,* Syracuse University Press, 1982.

> This study's introduction, its chapter on *Long Day's Journey into Night,* and its appendix focused on the play's motifs offer solid help in interpreting the play.

Pfister, Joel. "The Cultural Web in O'Neill's *Journey,"* in *Staging Depth: Eugene O'Neill and the Politics of Psychological Discourse,* University of North Carolina Press, 1995, pp. 203-15.

> Relates Mary from *Long Day's Journey into Night* to Ophelia in Shakespeare's *Hamlet* and Annie Keeney in O'Neill's earlier play, *Ile*.

Raleigh, John Henry. "O'Neill's *Long Day's Journey into Night* and New England Irish-Catholicism," *Partisan Review,* Vol. 26, no. 4, Fall, 1959, pp. 573-92.

> A helpful background study that relates the "dualism of religion-blasphemy" that permeates the play to Catholicism and Irish myth.

Milton Keynes UK
Ingram Content Group UK Ltd.
UKHW031416211124
2969UKWH00008B/183